Journey

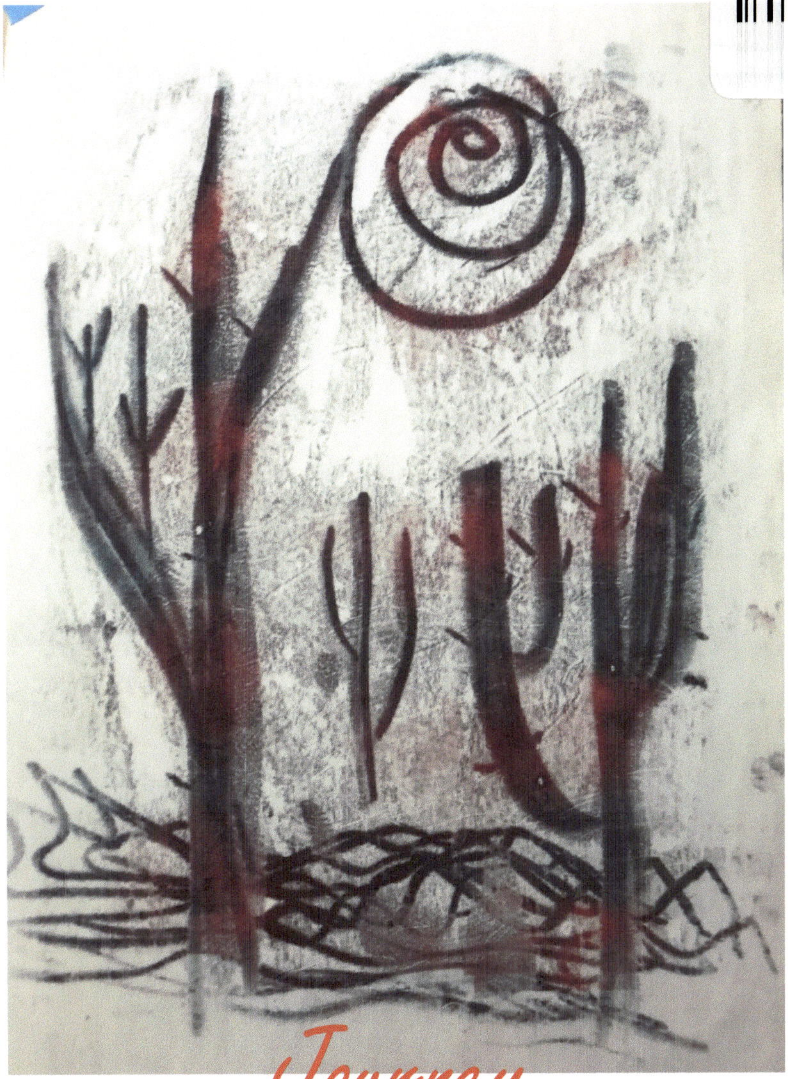

A Journal of Watercolor Mandala and Verse

by Olivia Maria Latiano, SND

"When I come to the end
I am still with you."

This line from the psalm is my hope.
I am never alone.

The psalmist was counting
the thoughts of God
and this was her experience:

to be with God
even when she came to the end of her understanding of God.

To feel the presence and care
of the ONE she cannot contain

and yet
who abides
within
her

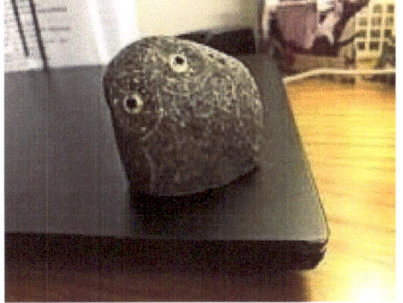

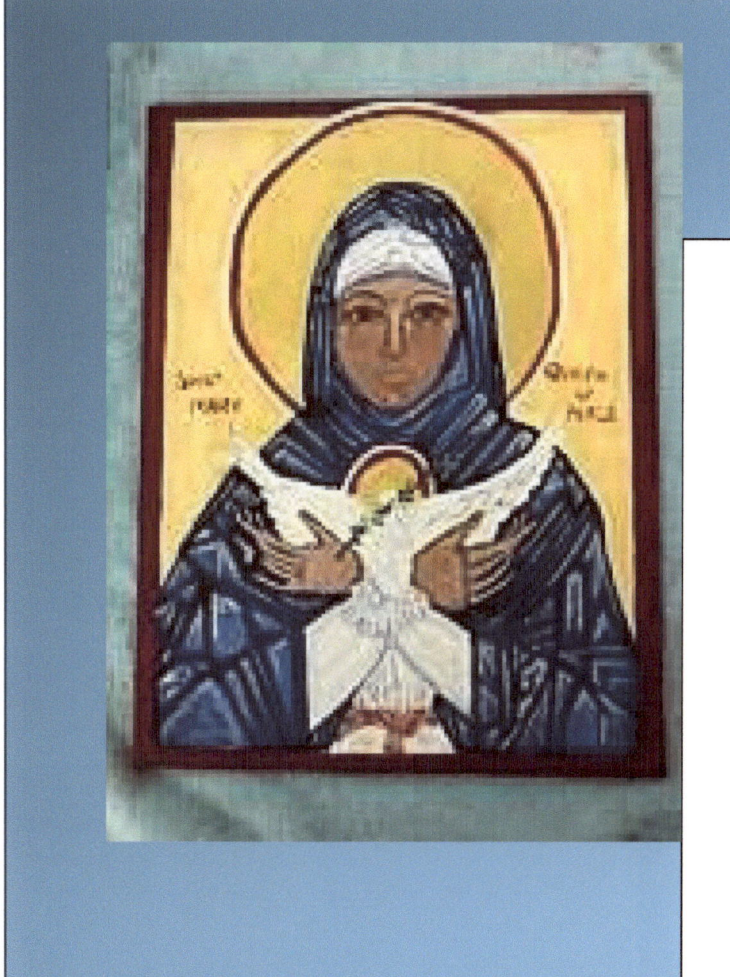

Annunciation

Announcing

Annotating

Answering

Agonizing

Allowing

Amnio

Alive

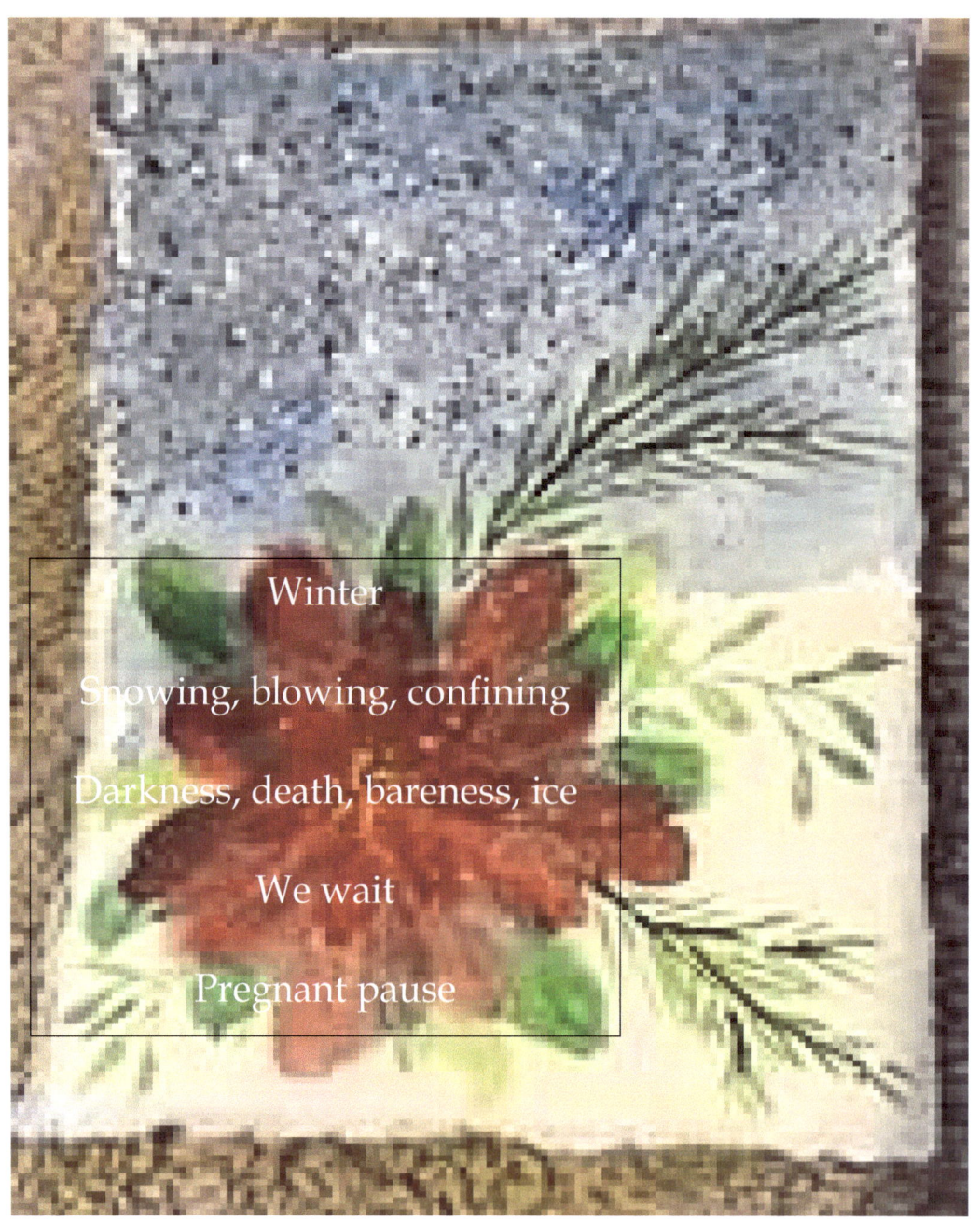

Winter

Snowing, blowing, confining

Darkness, death, bareness, ice

We wait

Pregnant pause

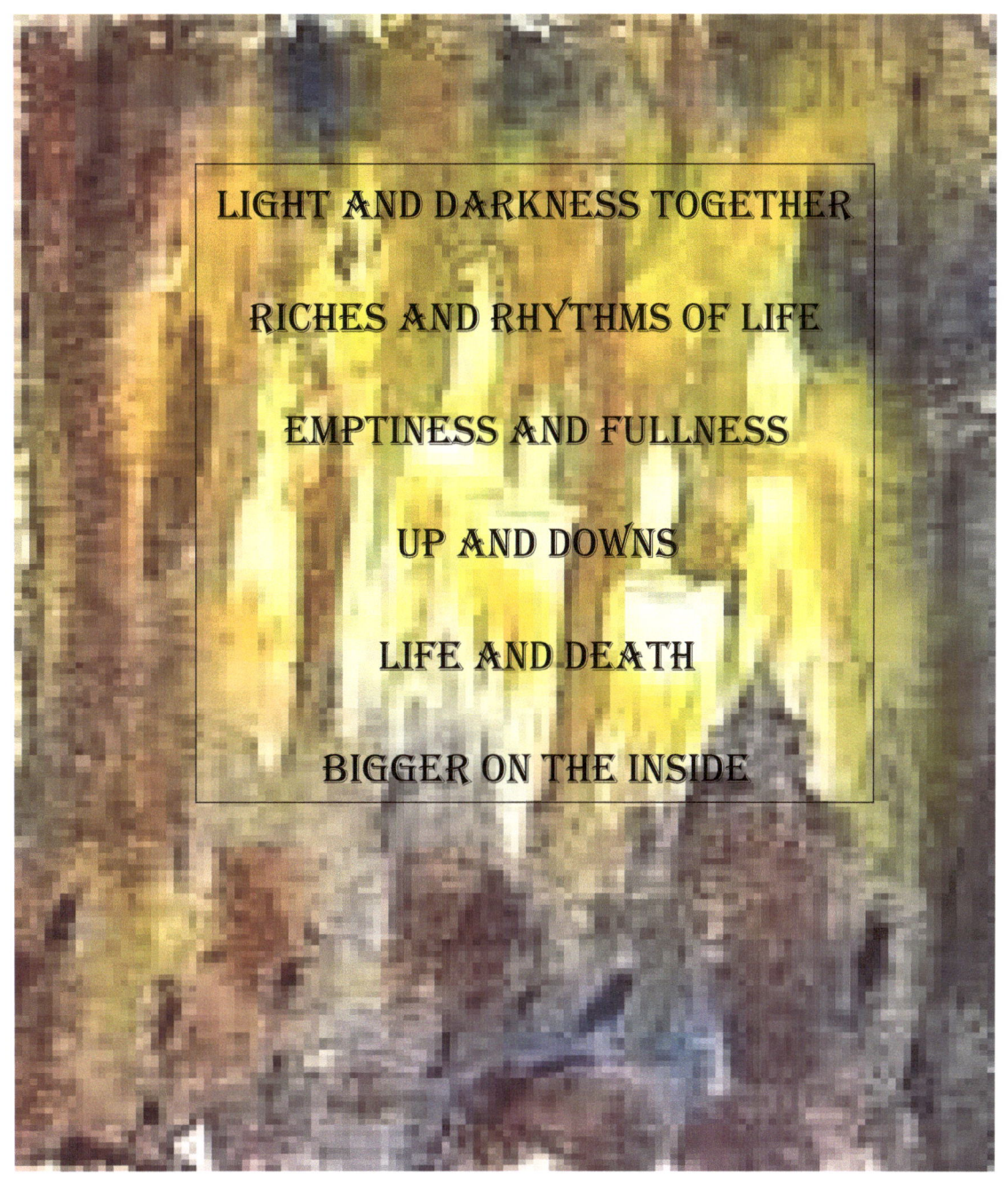

LIGHT AND DARKNESS TOGETHER

RICHES AND RHYTHMS OF LIFE

EMPTINESS AND FULLNESS

UP AND DOWNS

LIFE AND DEATH

BIGGER ON THE INSIDE

You are here
And you are coming

You are here
Because you inspirit all creation

And you are coming
Because if you didn't
We would put you up on a shelf
    or hang you on a wall
    or on a holy card
    or in a box in church

Oh! Wait we...

But you are coming anyway.

And you are here
Because you are timeless
And you are coming
Because we are not.

You are here
because you are Love
And you are coming
Because you love
Us.

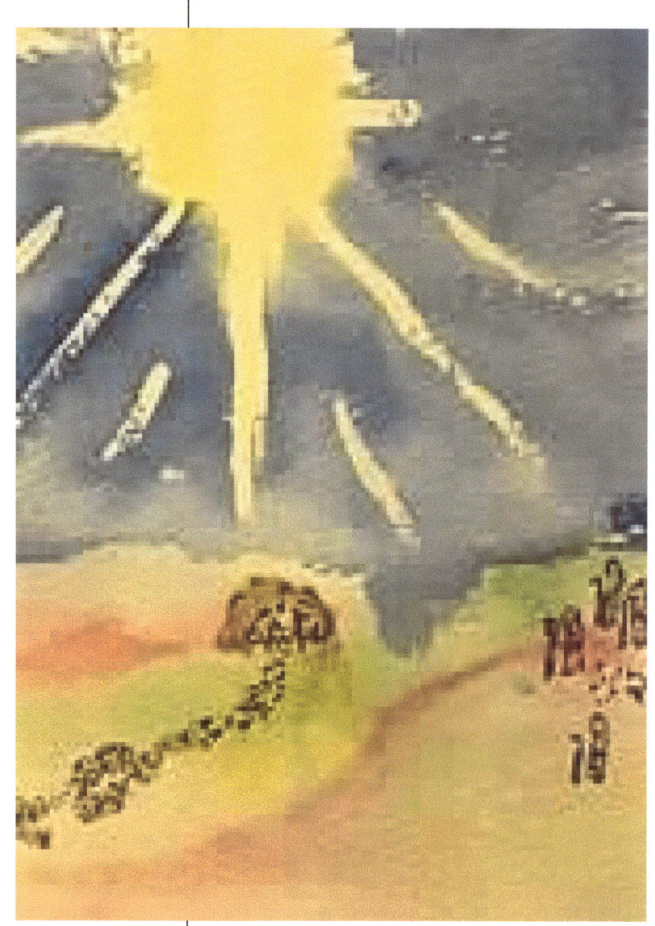

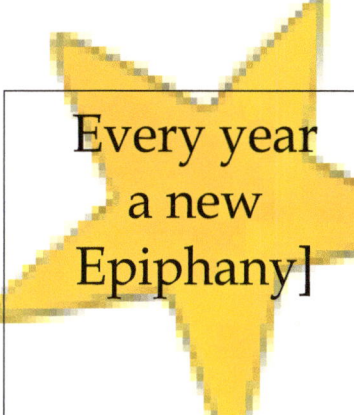

Every year
a new
Epiphany]

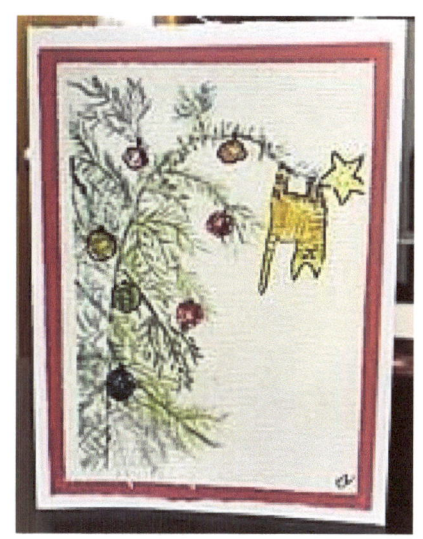

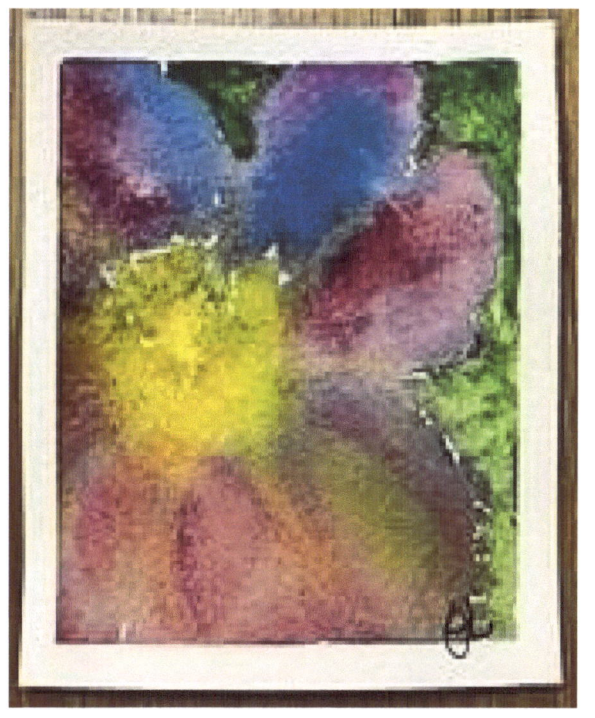

Why not
Welcome
the new year.

One day
at a time

Each day
new beginning.

Possibilities

One of many
New starts

What Epiphany today?

Awake at 3:30
coughing and wheezing.
Christmas lights my consolation

Christ has come
Filling the universe from its birth
From HIS birth

Students of the universe
From the Land of sunrise, (Star rise)
Bringing gifts of life and death.

His gift: his Self
All of Time and Space
We, his companions

Time And Relative Dimensions In Space
Bigger on the inside
Room for all.

Who is the God who made you and saves you.
The merciful One

Who answers prayers in God's time
Who desires union
Who is present in all circumstances

Desired or not God will be present.
We manufacture God's anger out of our own.

The all-patient One for whom 1000 years is like a day.
The Artist ever creating in the artist's own image

Green as the grass,
Black as the storm clouds

Soft as a kitten,
Solid as the mountains
Cool as the breeze,
Hot as the sun

Mysterious and ever-changing as the moon.
Refreshing as the flowing fountain
Nourishing as the fertile fields.
A passionate Spouse,
Protective Mother
Provident Father,
Faithful Friend.

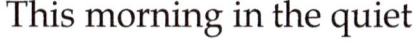

This morning in the quiet

Whatever terrible destruction
And extinction
Awaits us,
The human race,

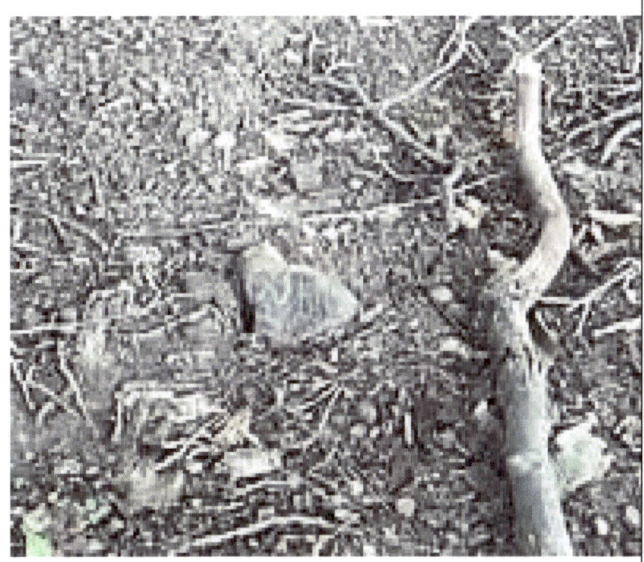

Peace is with You,
With us.

I don't like thinking we will lose,
We will die,
We will be destroyed,
The human race will
Become extinct.

And yet
There it is

So why not live
In the face of that.

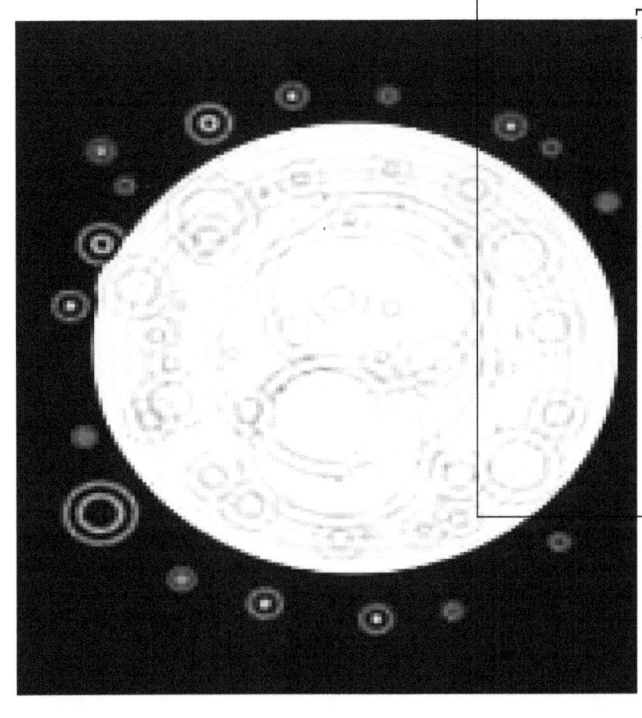

I am a complex, complicated person
(The beloved of God)
Layer upon swirling layer
Immersed in love
Though holding myself apart from love
Unsuccessfully, by the grace of God
The source of my being
"SOURCE AND SUMMIT"

Does that make me a holy liturgy
(not all to myself)
Struggling to give in to consecration
To submit to the miraculous
Amid the everyday

And the Everyperson
"THIS IS MY BODY"
(your body, our body)
THIS IS MY
(your, our)
BLOOD

The altar is stripped.
Emptied
of anything but essence
The sanctuary has nothing
but its sanctity.
The ambo has no book
to make it sacred
The altar has no victim
for sacrifice.

This is Jesus tonight
Emptied of anything
but his Father's will:
His essence.

Nothing added.
No success.
No ministry.
No disciples.

No wisdom to share
Save himself.

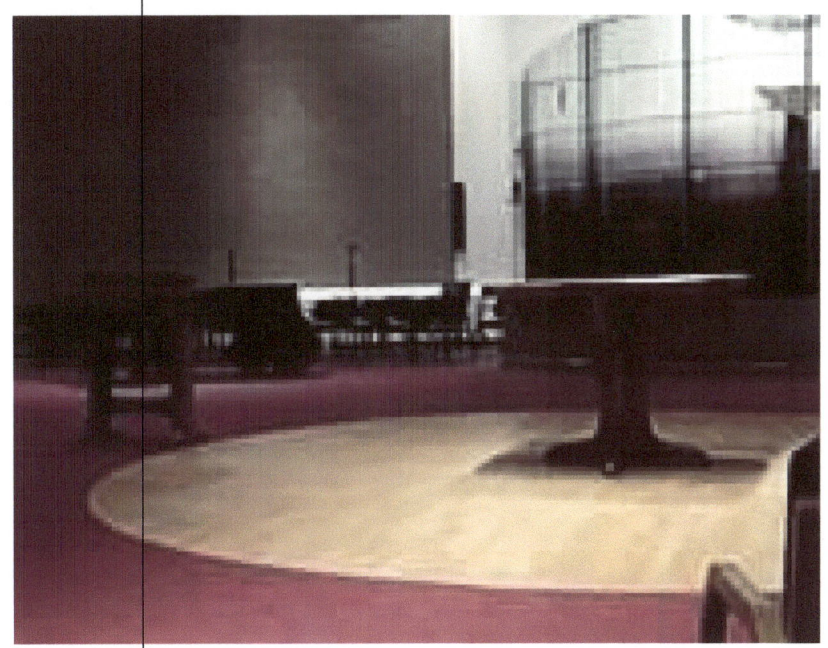

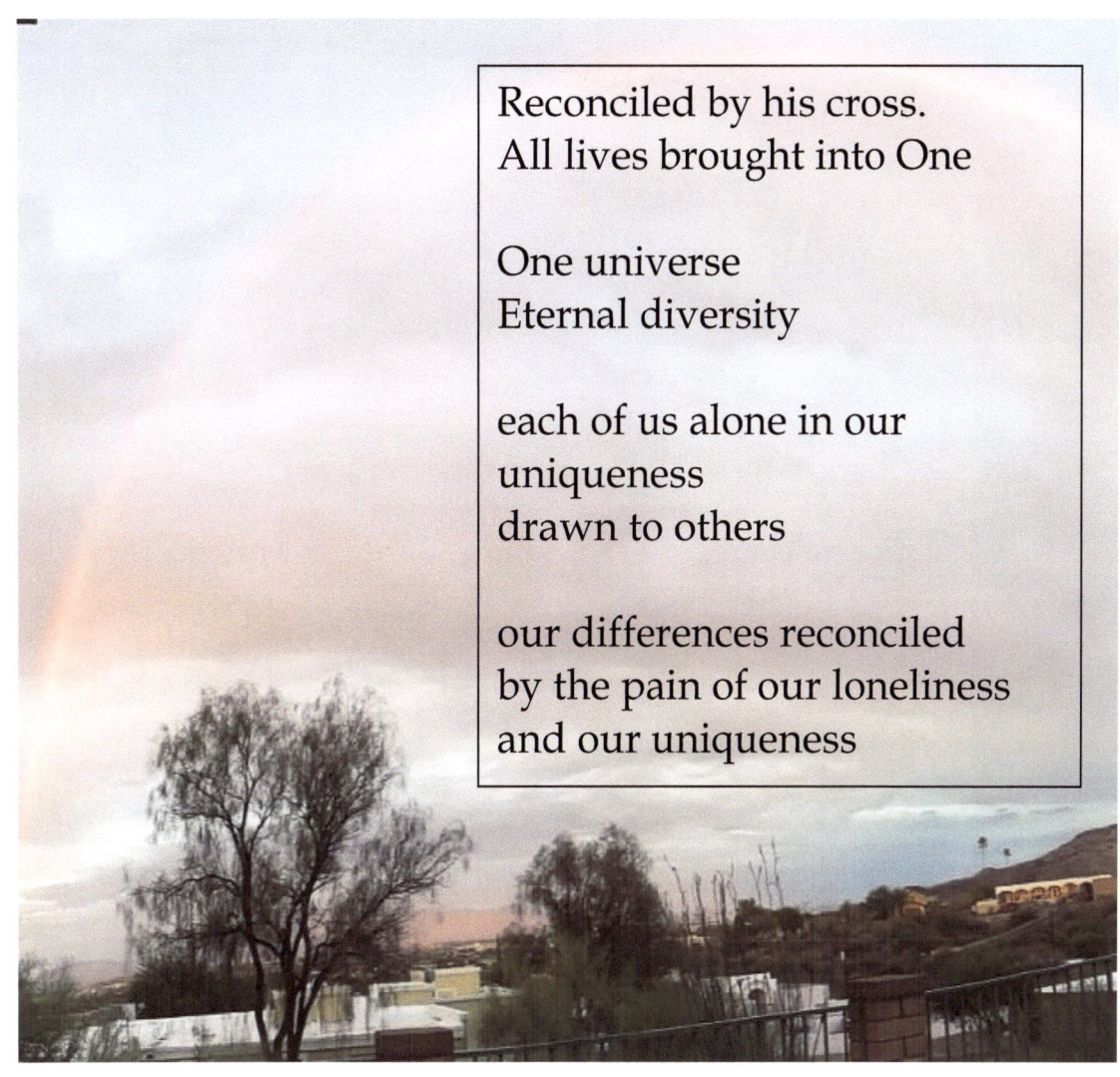

Reconciled by his cross.
All lives brought into One

One universe
Eternal diversity

each of us alone in our
uniqueness
drawn to others

our differences reconciled
by the pain of our loneliness
and our uniqueness

Emmaus Wednesday

Where shall I go?

Christ is risen, ALLELUIA!

To my inner room,
There a pilgrim
To a strange and mysterious
place.
But not alone.

open to hope
open to mystery
open to resurrection
open to the new
        the unexpected
        the impossible

Peace, it is I.
Do not be afraid.

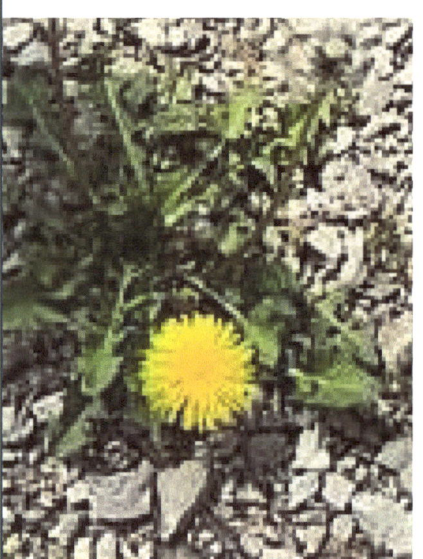

Unconditional love.

What matters?

Nothing but the two of us?

Everything including Everybody.

Judgement? no.

Greater and lesser? Never.

Perfection? Ahhhhhh... letting go!

And Acceptance, yes.

As you are.

All.
Ever.
Now.
And Evermore.

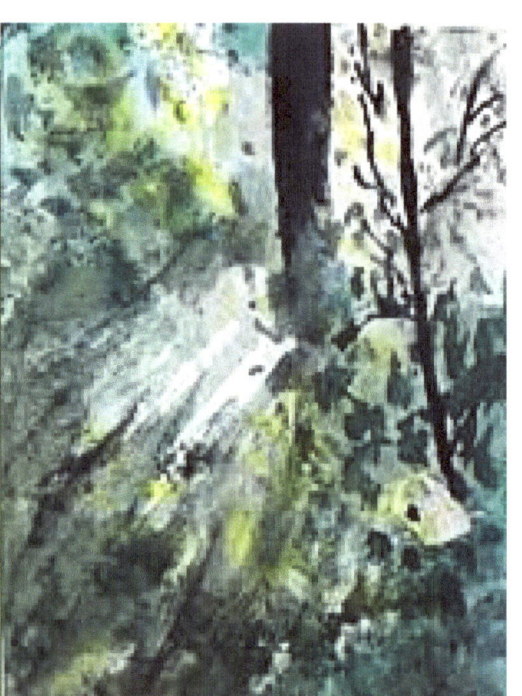

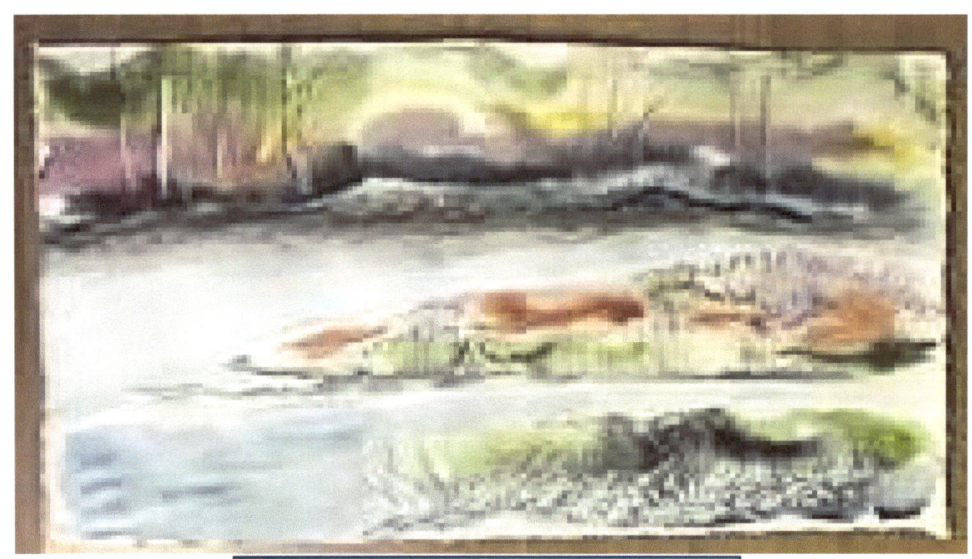

Water Spirit
Moisten our spirits
Carry us
Soak us
Drown us
In your compassion

Wind Spirit
Blow through us
Blow us up
Explode Among us
Lift us, kite us through
your sky
Pierce us with your mercy

Sacred Heart

Broken Heart
Given Heart

Heart of Creation
Of the Universe
The Multiverse?

Broken and healed
Dead and raised to new life

New growth from death and
destruction
from loss and loneliness

Desperation and depression,
Betrayal and failure

Love to love
Heart to heart

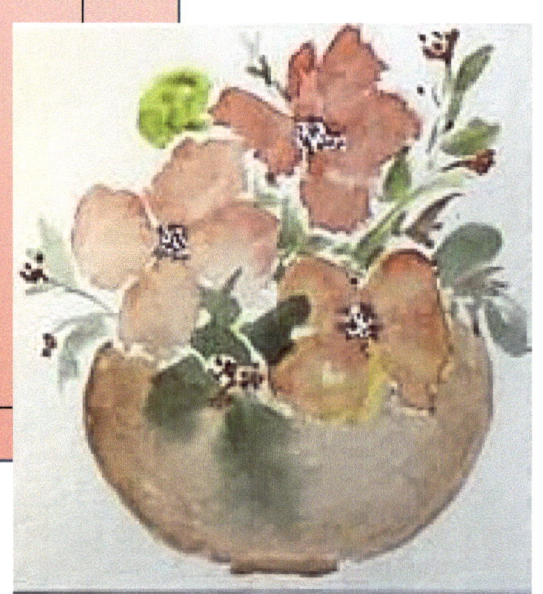

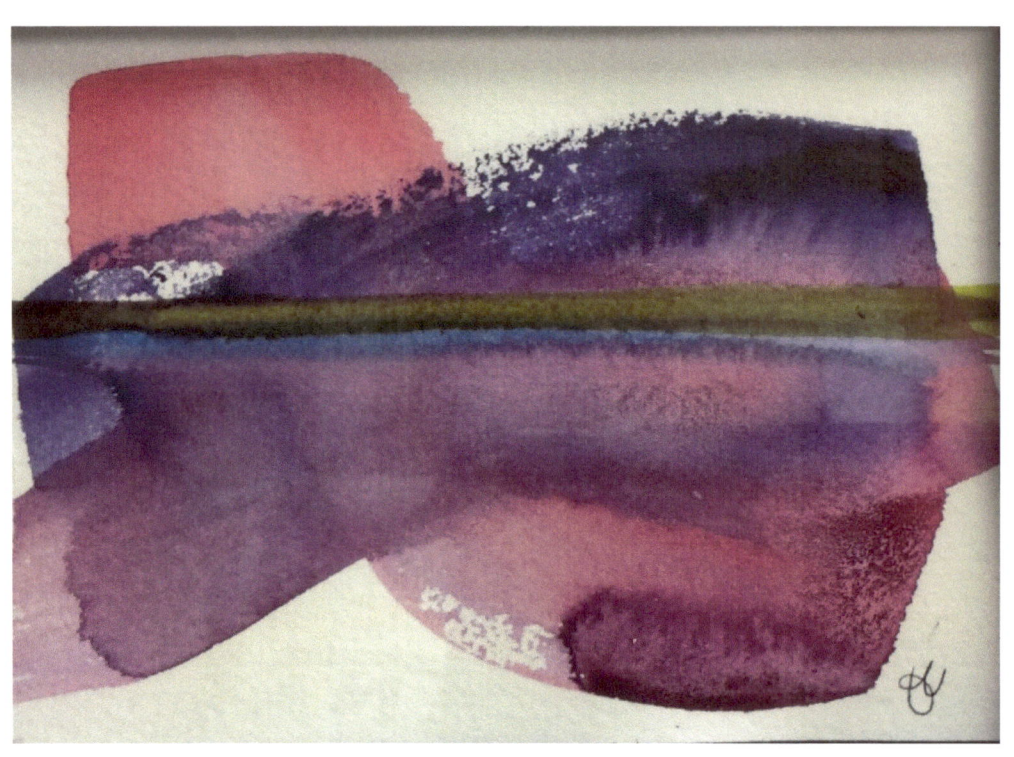

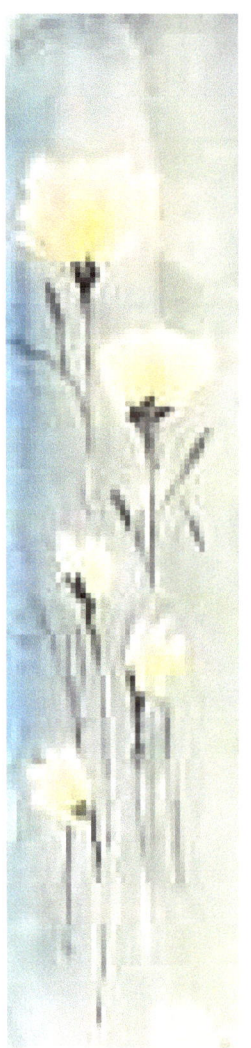

Leave sadness to the world.
We who are of God
should be lighthearted.
(Leonard of Port Maurice)

Give me a sense of humor, Lord,
and something to laugh about.
(Thomas More)

When one loves,
everything is joy.
(Theresa de los Andes)

Have patience with all the world,
but with yourself first.
(Frances de Sales)

Nothing is far from God
(Monica)

A friend is called a guardian of love
or as some would have it,
a guardian of the spirit itself
Nothing more useful is sought after;
nothing more difficult is discovered;
nothing more sweet experienced,
and nothing more profitable possessed.
(Aelred)

Your son went down
from the heights of his divinity
to the depths of our humanity.
Can anyone's heart
remain closed and hardened after this.
(Catherine of Siena)

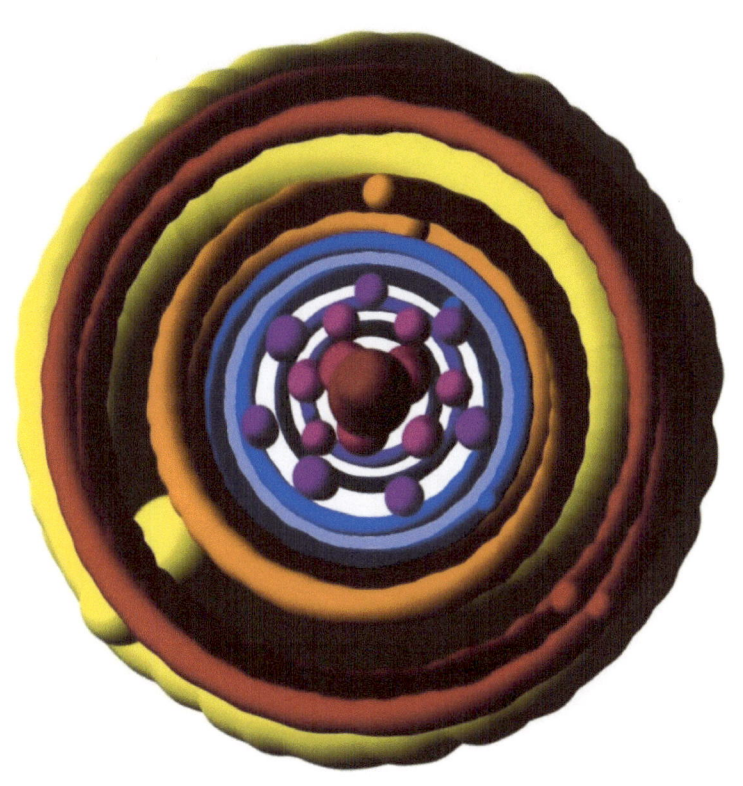

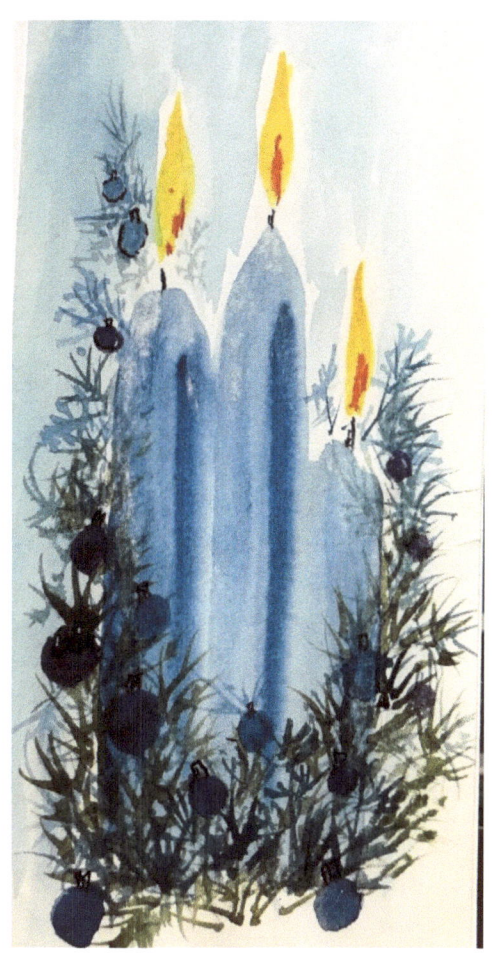

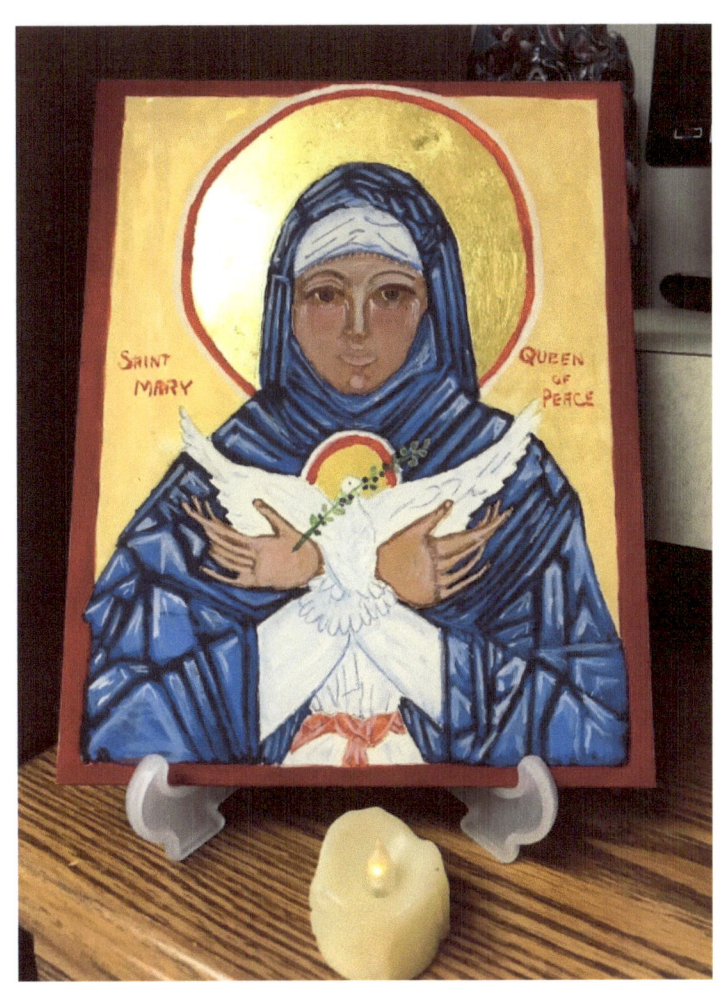

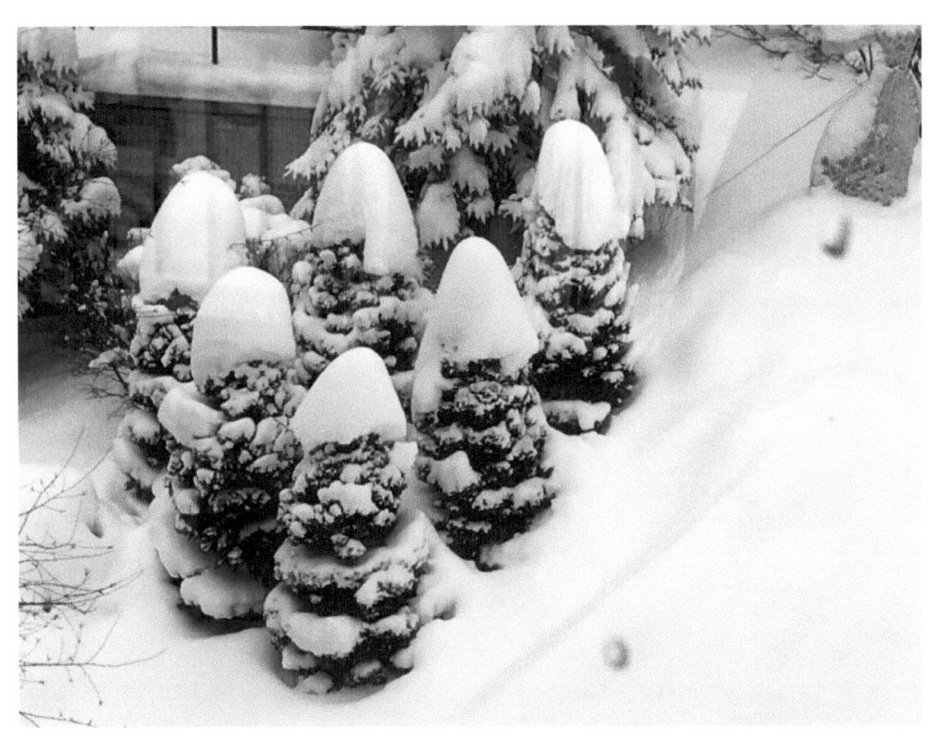

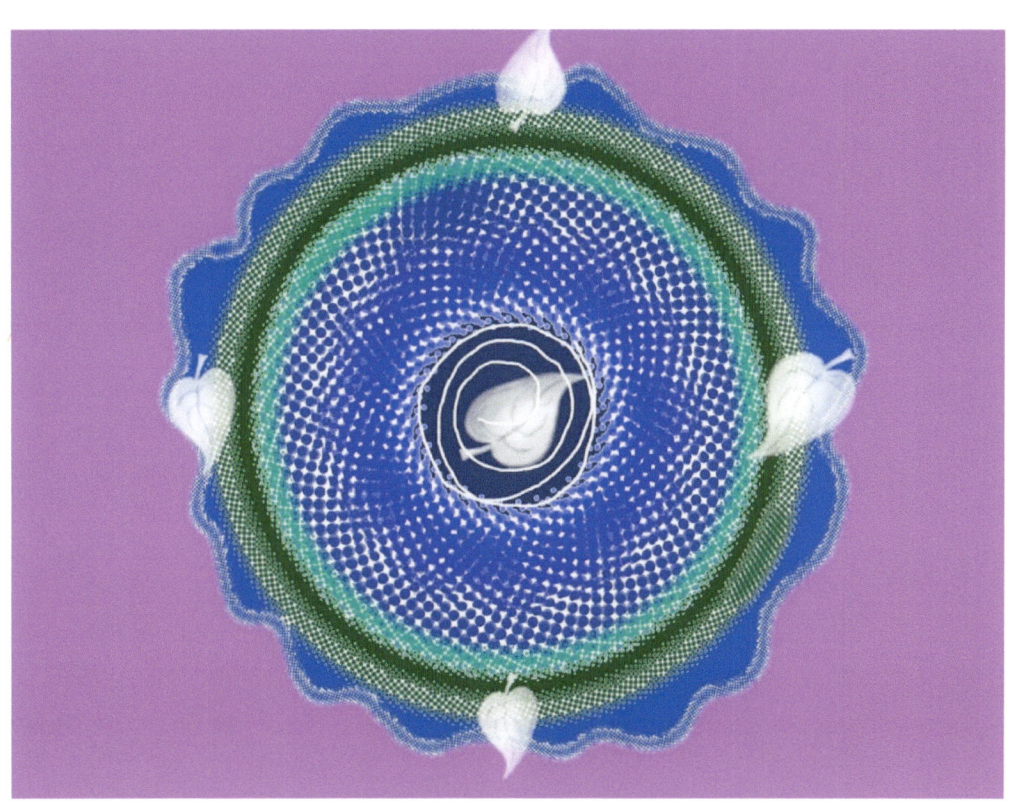